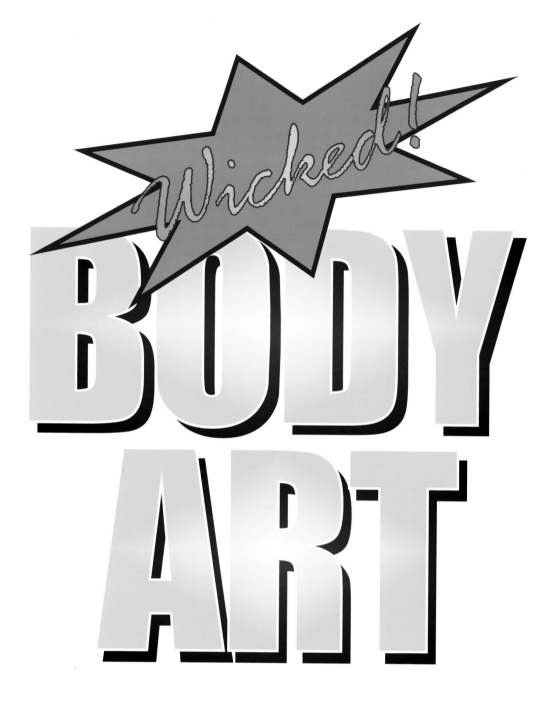

Wicked! BODY ART

AN ESSENTIAL GUIDE TO PAINTING AND DECORATING YOUR BODY FROM TOP TO TOE!

Susannah Rose

Acknowledgments:
Special thanks to the students and staff of Gateway College in Leicester.
Models: James Baker, Carmen Jones, Natasha Patel, Dominic Zaman, Gabi Beswic, Mathew Peers, Vashali Parmar, Adam Ray, Lindsay Findlay, Olga Dubrova, Danielle Baker, Tim Dodd, Farhana Kadri

This edition first published in the United Kingdom in 2001 by Caxton Editions
20 Bloomsbury Street
London WC1B 3JH
a member of the Caxton Publishing Group

© Copyright 2001 Caxton Publishing Group

Designed and Produced for Caxton Editions by
Open Door Limited
Rutland, UK
Colour separation: GA Graphics Stamford
Digital imagery © copyright PhotoDisc Inc.

Title: Wicked Body Art
ISBN: 1 84067 277 3

Notice: Body art materials should be used with care and manufacturer's guidelines adhered to at all times. Therefore the publisher and producers of this book accept no responsibility for any damage caused by the use of practices contained in this book.

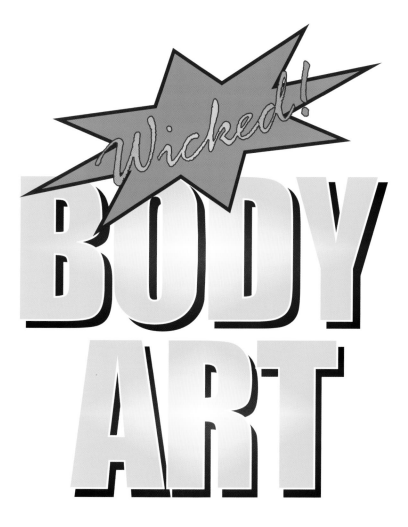

Wicked!

BODY ART

Susannah Rose

CAXTON EDITIONS

Contents

Contents

Introduction

The Art of painting the body has been explored for centuries, and has been used in all of the ancient cultures as a way of expressing the personality of the individual. There are many ways of creating exciting new looks – which can be worn by anyone to varying degrees – so whether you want to go for subtle evening elegance or for show stopping dramatic effect, the possibilities are endless. The examples in this book can be dressed up or down depending on whether you want to wear them during the day or in a club at night. During the summer, heavy jewellery or makeup can be uncomfortable and impractical on the beach, so a good way of adorning the body is with henna, which is semi-permanent and will withstand a dip in the sea! If you are going out to a club or party, you can try some of the eye catching designs using body inks and paints, finished off of course with a touch of glitter!

Inspiration

What inspires you is very individual. You can draw upon ancient symbols and images from India, Egypt, Aztec – anywhere that takes your fancy! Or you can go for a futuristic look, influenced by Sci-fi films and comics. What is important though, is that you experiment and have fun with the ideas that you have. Creating and working on the design should be as much fun as wearing it! Many famous stars express themselves at opening nights or premieres by wearing some form of beautiful body adornment.

Look at photographs in fashion magazines, especially catwalk pictures, where innovative designers really push the dramatic element of body art.

Animal Prints

Animal prints are fun to take inspiration from. You can create bracelets of tiger stripes or zebra print. Simple to create, simply start with a solid block of colour and then layer darker stripes over the top.

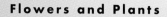

Flowers and Plants

Flowers and plants are always popular. Their lovely flowing lines lend themselves well to freehand designs. Certain plants and flowers are deeply symbolic.

Astrological

Choose a symbol that is personal to you (see p. 70).

Futuristic

Look at sci-fi films, makeup artists always explore their imaginations to bring a fantasy to life (see p. 89).

Vintage

Old-fashioned designs are making a comeback. Try looking at old sailor's tattoos for inspiration.

Henna Body Painting

A Beginners Guide

*I*f you can doodle, you can easily use henna! Although henna can be messy, the results are longer lasting than inks or transfers. It is worth the extra time, and the design will last for at least 3-4 weeks. Before you start, however it is worth bearing a few things in mind. Firstly, Henna is a natural product and has been used for thousands of years, however, it is always worth doing a skin test first, this will determine if you are sensitive to the henna and will also give you an indication of how dark the finished design will be.

To do a skin test, apply a small amount of paste to the inside of your arm, wait for ten minutes and then scrape it off. After 24 hours, check the area again. If there is no soreness or itching you should be safe to carry on.

Henna stains pretty much anything, so make sure that you protect your clothing, hair and any other pale fabrics around you whilst you apply the henna and also whilst waiting for it to dry!

Henna application is time consuming and always takes slightly longer than you think. If you want a henna design for a particular occasion it is probably a good idea to apply it a couple of days before the special day. That way you know that you have plenty of time and you won't be tempted to rush the process. Hopefully you will avoid any messy accidents!

11

Buying Henna

Henna is available everywhere these days. Try health food shops or ethnic stores as well as the Internet. You can choose from pure henna powder or pre mixed tubes of paste. Henna Kits that include tubes of paste, oil and stencils are also available. It is up to you which to go for, but as a general guide;
Pre-mixed tubes are easier to use, and come in a wide variety of shades, but the colours do not always last as long. Henna powder has to be prepared and for the best result needs

to be left overnight, but the colour is normally stronger and more vibrant. You will also need diluted Mehandi oil or Eucalyptus essential oil to set your design. Remember to do a skin test with essential oils, and always follow the correct dilution. If you have very sensitive skin, try using baby oil instead of essential oil.

Applicators

Plastic bottles with a various size nozzle

attachments are available. These are the

easiest types of applicator to use.

Otherwise you can improvise with an icing

bag, ready bought or make your own.

Simply take a piece of greaseproof paper

and roll it into a cone shape. Fill

the cone with about 3

tablespoons of

paste, then fold

over the end and secure

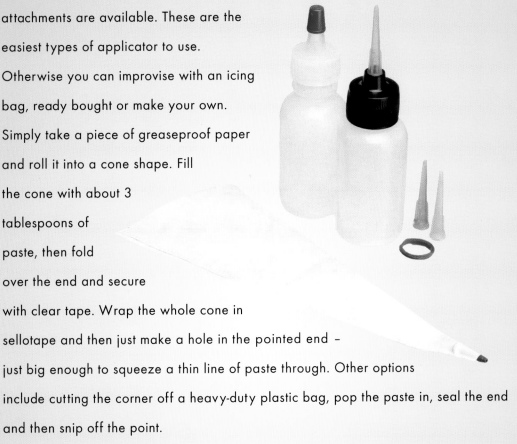

with clear tape. Wrap the whole cone in

sellotape and then just make a hole in the pointed end –

just big enough to squeeze a thin line of paste through. Other options

include cutting the corner off a heavy-duty plastic bag, pop the paste in, seal the end

and then snip off the point.

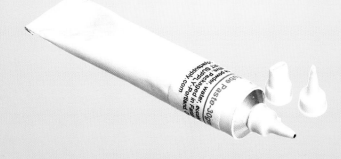

Mixing up and using henna paste

You will need some henna powder, the best type is available from Indian stores and it is usually cheaper than fancy boxed henna. Make sure that you sift it first to get rid of large lumps and leaves. This will also help you to create smoother and finer lines.

Put a tablespoon of henna powder in a plastic bowl.

Add a couple of teaspoons of strained fresh lemon juice to the henna powder.

Mix together with a plastic spoon, adding more lemon juice until you get a thick paste.

To darken the final colour add a couple of drops of clove oil, but if you have sensitive skin, please do a skin test before hand to make sure that you do not develop an allergic reaction to this essential oil.

Mix thoroughly and then cover the bowl with cling film and allow it to stand in a warm place for 6 hours.

14

After six hours, remove the cling film and add a teaspoon of honey, a little more lemon juice (or strong black coffee for a darker colour) and stir.

Repeat until the surface of the henna has a reflective sheen on it. The consistency should be soft and smooth, but not runny.

The paste is now ready for use. Fill your chosen applicator with the mixture and try a few practice lines and doodles on a piece of paper.

You also need to prepare a protective coating for the finished henna design.

This can be applied to the dry henna to seal it and keep it moist so that the colour penetrates the skin effectively.

Put some lemon juice into a glass, add a teaspoon of white sugar and stir until it has dissolved. Soak a cotton wool ball in the mixture and dab it onto the finished design.

Creating a design

You are now ready to start creating your design.

1 **Choose the area you want to work on. Wash the area thoroughly with soap to remove any oils, perfumes or moisturisers from the skin, then pat dry.**

2 **Sketch out the design using brown eyeliner, or if you are using a stencil, carefully press down on the skin – making sure that it sticks well without lifting at the edges.**

3 **Start to apply the henna as though you were icing a cake. Keep the lines smooth and flowing. If you make a mistake, use a cotton wool bud to wipe off the henna.**

4 **Draw the edges first, then fill in the solid areas.**

5 If you notice that the henna is beginning to dry and crack, carefully dab the lemon/sugar solution onto the henna surface. This will moisten and protect the henna.

6 When finished, gently coat the whole design in the syrup mixture and allow to dry. In order to develop the deepest colour, the henna needs to stay moist on the skin for at least 8 hours, or longer if possible.

7 You will need to cover the design to prevent it from getting smudged. Just apply a layer of tissue paper, then hold this is place by wrapping it round twice with a strip of cling film and then, if necessary, secure with masking tape.

8 When you are ready to remove the henna, scrape it off and gently rub a cotton wool ball soaked in Mehandi oil over the design, to remove any excess paste. Try not to wash the area for at least 24 hours, to allow the full colour to develop.

A warning about coloured hennas

Any product that calls itself black henna is using a different ingredient than henna to achieve its colour. The leaves of the henna plant naturally give a dark orange colour. Some products calling themselves black henna contain an extremely toxic substance that may cause severe burning and are best avoided. If a street painter is using black henna, it is probably best to not have a design done at all. Make sure that if you purchase a black henna it is from a reputable supplier, always follow the manufacturer's instructions for use and always do a skin test before using it. Many coloured hennas only take a couple of hours to colour your skin successfully and there are some good safe makes available, but it is worth shopping around. There are are some suppliers details in the back of this book, which may be helpful. Natural Henna does take at least 6-8 hours to stain. Anything else is chemically enhanced. If you do get a black henna burn, go to the doctor as soon as possible to get it treated.

Remember, if you are at all unsure about the product it is best to avoid it.

Essential oils

Caution should also be taken when using essential oils. Always remember to use them to their correct dilution. Always follow the manufacturers guidelines for dilution and use, but if you are still unsure take the time to find out what you need to know before proceeding – never take a chance.

Finally, make sure you know what you are doing before you begin – remember, henna stains as soon as it is applied! Getting ready to start painting is as important as the painting itself.

Henna aftercare

The colour you see when you first remove the paste is not the full colour; this appears around 24 hours later and will be much stronger.

Try not to wash new henna motifs, at least for a day or so. This will improve their life-span.

Using a moisturiser on the motif will help extend its life. Do not apply more than twice a day, however.

Coloured Inks, Paints & Dyes

You may prefer to experiment with some of the other alternatives to henna that are on the market. In many ways, these are easier to use and much less time consuming. Also, if you are a beginner and you make a mistake, you can simply wipe the paint off and start again!

Body Inks

Cosmetic Inks tend to be alcohol based, so that they are normally fairly smudge resistant. You can find virtually any colour of the rainbow, as well as metallic and UV glow in the dark colours, which are excellent for clubs.

Remember to cleanse the area that you wish to paint first to ensure that the ink clings to the skin.

Application is very simple, just paint them on with a fine paintbrush, it is a good idea to have brushes of varying sizes.

Use baby oil to clean the brushes – most inks are alcohol based and so you need alcohol swabs or baby oil to remove them.

You have to work quickly, inks set almost immediately. A major advantage of inks is that you can layer colours to achieve texture and complex looking effects, although they really are simple to use! The designs last for 2-5 days – especially if you set the final design with a little talcum powder.

Body Paints

There are currently two types of body paint – grease and water based. Grease paint is better for all over body designs, it dries very quickly and a little goes a long way. Water based is much better for detailed work, it sets rather like water colour paint and is particularly good for children, because it is so gentle on the skin. Water based body paint is available as dry blocks that you moisten or in bottles in a liquid form. The range of colours is endless and you can get some lovely metallic shades!

As with inks, application is very simple. You can use brushes or sponges. Try latex wedges cut into star shapes with gold body paint.

24

Use a wet sponge to fill in large areas,

layer the paint to achieve the right intensity.

You can blend colours with your fingers or with a damp brush.

Set the finished design with talcum powder.

Designs are very temporary, they will last for a day and can be easily

washed off with soap and water.

Body dye

Body dye designs will last for a couple of days and, again, are very easy to apply. A lot of major makeup companies produce temporary tattoo kits in the summer, which normally contain 2-3 bottles or tubes of the gel-like dye and setting liquid.

Cleanse the skin thoroughly before use.

Apply the dye, similar in texture to henna, to the skin.

You can use water to dilute the dye for detailed work.

Apply the setting liquid and allow to dry for 40 minutes.

Gently rub or peel off the dried gel-film, to reveal the finished design.

The design can be removed with soap and water.

26

Temporary tattoos

Temporary tattoos are a convenient way of wearing body art without the permanence (or pain!) of getting a real one. They can also help you decide whether or not you want to get the real thing done, and in this day and age, piercing and tattooing are much more popular and accessible than ever before. Fake tattoos come in all sorts of designs and are very easy to use.

28

1 Cleanse the skin with soap and water before you apply the tattoo. If possible exfoliate the area to be tattooed using a little sugar and soap. Ensure skin is completely dry.

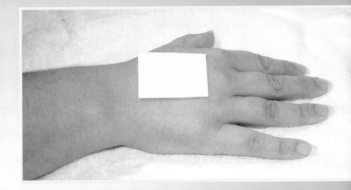

2 Place the tattoo face down on the skin.

3 Using a damp cloth, apply pressure onto the design. Hold for a couple of minutes, then carefully slide off the top paper revealing the design underneath.

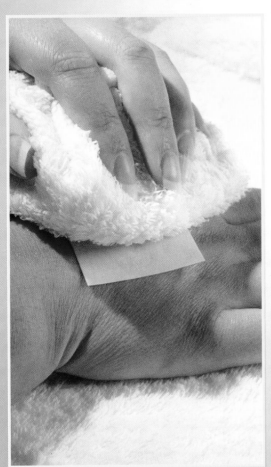

4 Rinse very gently and allow to dry.

5 Usually a temporary tattoo will last for around five days. Use baby oil to remove them.

Bindis

Bindis are little pieces of felt or plastic, which have ornate designs on them. Usually worn on the forehead, they are a beautiful and yet simple way of adding glamour to evening wear. You can go for classic elegant or clubbing outrageous! Bindis can be bought from market stalls and accessory shops – although they will vary in price greatly. You can even make your own.

30

Temporary Tattoos, Bindis, Stick-on Gems & Glitter

You will need:

1. Some small pieces of felt or plastic coated card (you can get metallic colours from any art shop)

2. Some tiny beads and sequins – any colour that you like!

3. A glitter glue pen or fabric glue pens (you can get these in all colours, including gold, silver and fluorescent)

4. Strong, clear drying, fabric glue

5. A pair of tweezers

6. Sharp scissors

7. Eyelash adhesive (for gluing the bindi to your skin)

31

First, cut out the shape of the bindi from the card or felt. (If you are using felt, it is a good idea to stick this onto some card, using clear adhesive, first). Classic shapes are ovals, teardrops or circles, but you may prefer something more contemporary – perhaps a square, diamond or rectangle.

Place the shape onto some card using blue tack to hold it still while you are working on it.

Using tweezers, glue the beads and sequins onto the bindi with clear drying glue. Wait for it to dry.

4 Using glitter glue or fabric pens, add detail to the design and embellish the edge of the bindi.

5 Allow to dry for a couple of hours. When you want to wear it, remove the blue tack from bindi, cover the back in eyelash adhesive, wait for one minute until the glue becomes tacky and then simply stick it onto clean dry skin!

Stick-on Gems

These are tiny, self-adhesive, gems that can be worn all over the face and body to create magical effects. Again, you can make your own by using eyelash adhesive with coloured beads or sequins.

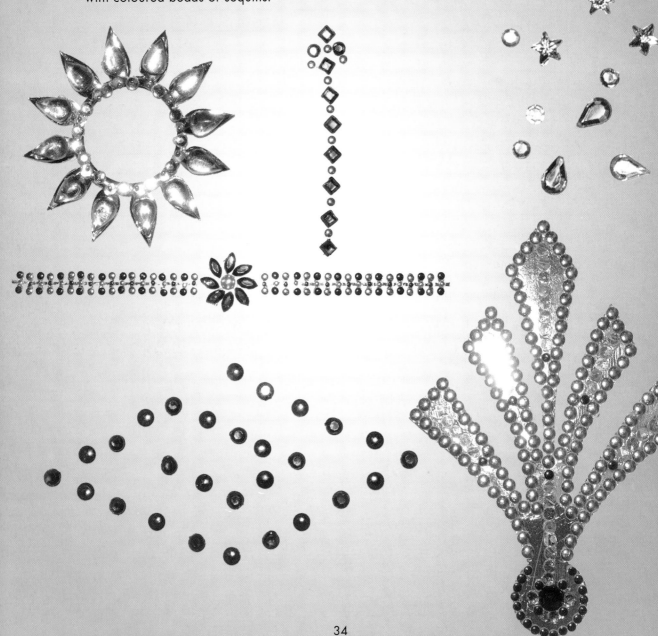

Glitter

Glitter comes in all sorts of types and colours, from subtle baby pink to dramatic

black and red. Use with petroleum jelly to

highlight cheekbones and eyebrows, or

mix with moisturiser and apply all over

the body for fairy tale shimmer.

You can buy glitter loose or

in a gel base. The gel type

is easier to use, but dries

out quickly, so make

sure that you always

keep the lid on tightly.

Apply itwith a makeup

brush or your fingertips and layer the effect. You can use it in your hair, but make sure

that you mix it with some hair gel or mousse, and then spray with a fine mist of

hairspray to stop it sprinkling everywhere!

35

Iridescent Powders

These are little pots of colourful powder that have a two-tone sheen – rather like a butterfly wing. It is always worth experimenting with these, as the effects can be quite stunning. Some can be mixed with moisturiser or water and applied wet, for a darker colour.

Conventional Makeup

Don't forget conventional makeup, eyeliner pens and liquids are always useful for marking out designs or adding detail.

Body Art Projects

Diamond Eyelash Line

These glittery eyelash lines have been worn by some of the most glamorous people in the world. Seen on catwalks, cosmetic houses brought out expensive kits to create the look. You can do it yourself quite easily, using tiny diamantes. With a little practice you can build up the amount of gems that you use. Start with around 7-8 gems per eye, or if you prefer you can use just 4-5 gems at the very edge of the eyes. You can vary this look by using different coloured eyeliner and gems.

You will need:

Tiny diamante or plastic gems with a flat underside. These can be bought from any bead seller or sometimes from a haberdashery.

A tube of eyelash glue

Gold liquid eyeliner

A pair of tweezers

A wooden matchstick

First, apply any other makeup that you will be wearing – including mascara. The effect is much more dramatic if applied last of all and you don't want wet mascara smudging the little gems.

Carefully draw a thick line just above your eyelashes with the gold liquid liner. You can also use liquid water based body paint with a fine brush, just ask the retailer of the paint if it is suitable for this area first.

Allow to dry for a few minutes.

Squeeze a little of the eyelash adhesive out onto a plate and mix it with the matchstick – so that any bubbles are smoothed out. Eyelash adhesive dries quite quickly – so you will have to work fast.

Using tweezers, take a gem and gently coat the flat side. Press this onto the eyelid, just above the eyelash. Hold in place for a couple of seconds. Repeat with the rest, leaving tiny gaps between them. The eyelash glue will dry clear. Try not to blink too much until all of the gems are in place and dry.

The gems should stay in place for the whole evening – they may feel slightly strange at first, but as long as you use lightweight gems, they should not be too uncomfortable. If you have very sensitive eyes, you can modify this look by mixing glitter with under-eye gel and painting this on over the eyeliner instead of using gems.

When you want to remove the gems, just gently peel them off, using a little baby oil on a cotton wool ball to remove any last traces of eyelash adhesive.

Starry, Starry Eyes

This is a very easy effect to achieve and is particularly effective with a tan. Because it is quite dramatic, you probably won't need to wear any other makeup at all – which makes it a nice look for hot summer evenings.

You will need:

Gold glitter gel

Liquid gold water based body paint

A very fine paint brush

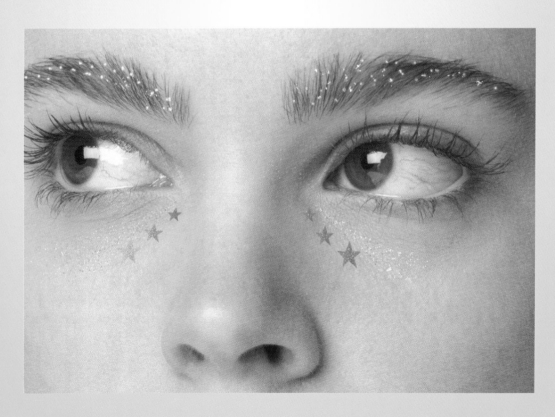

1 Lightly moisturise and then use a tissue to absorb any excess oil from the skin.

2 Using a fine brush, paint 3-4 tiny stars in a tear line underneath the eyes with the gold paint.

3 Just outside of the stars, draw a line in gold glitter gel to form a sunray.

4 Rub a small amount of glitter through your eyebrows with your finger.

5 To remove, simply wash off with soap and water.

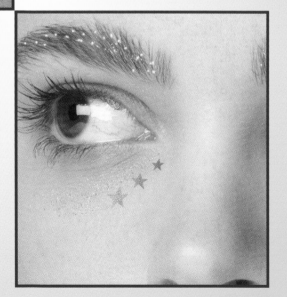

43

Oriental Neck Motif

In many cultures, the back of the neck has long been thought to be one of the most sensual parts of the body. As part of the elaborate dress ritual of the traditional Geisha, the back of the neck was painted with a lattice motif, which would offer a glimpse of bare skin underneath. For a more modern approach to this theme, find an oriental pattern, character, or motif which appeals to you and apply this to the back of your neck. A geometric design works best, placed in the middle of your neck to balance either side.

When worn with the hair gathered up into a chignon or bun, this design is guaranteed to turn heads.

You will need to get a friend to apply this for you.

44

For this design use henna for the outline and fill in with gold body paint or ink. Although you can prepare henna paste from scratch for this design, Pre-mixed natural henna paste, available in tubes with an applicator, would be better. If using coloured henna paste, you only need to leave it on for 2-3 hours for the stain to develop. For neck designs this is recommended; (you will probably smudge the neck area if the paste is left on overnight).

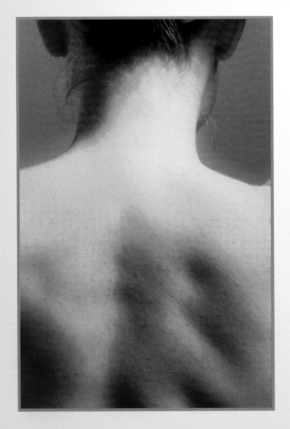

First cleanse the area and moisturise with a little baby oil. Make sure that you gather your hair up securely – henna stains everything that it comes into contact with, and the last thing that you want is a patch of different coloured hair at the back of your head!

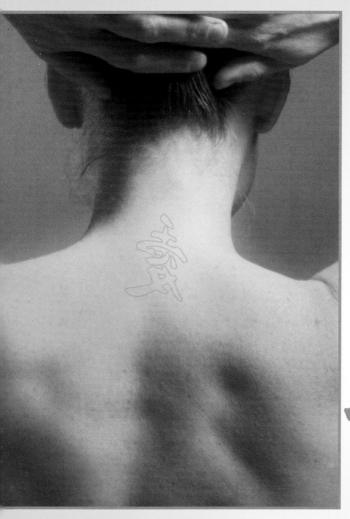

If you feel confident enough to draw the design freehand, do so using brown eyeliner pencil. If not, you may want to use the following method:

To transfer the design to the back of the neck, simply trace the design onto thin paper. Rub brown eyeliner onto the back of the paper and trim just around the design.

Using two short strips of surgical tape or two small plasters, secure the paper to the back of the neck. Use a pencil to trace the design through the paper – using firm, but gentle, pressure.

Remove the paper, taking care not to smudge the design. Eyeliner is very good for marking out designs with because it washes off without affecting the properties of the henna, but make sure that you only use light strokes. It is simply a guideline that you want. The rest is all about practising with the henna.

5 Draw the design out with the henna, using even lines. Try to keep the design clean. Use toothpicks and cotton wool buds to remove any mistakes or to adjust lines. Seal the henna with a light coating of sugar/lemon solution, dabbed on with a cotton wool ball.

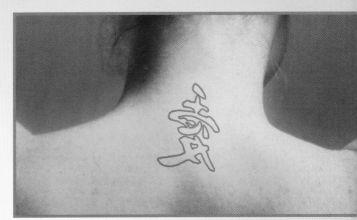

6 Allow to develop for 2-3 hours. The back of the neck is very warm, so the paste may dry out quite quickly. Use the solution to prevent this from happening.

7 After the henna has developed, scrape off and gently rub the design with a cotton wool ball soaked in Mehandi oil to remove the excess paste.

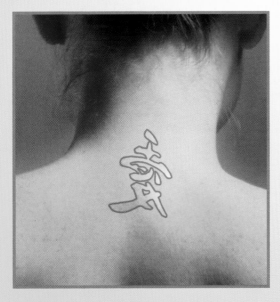

8 When the outline is complete, you can fill in the design using gold ink or paint. Use a medium size brush to do this, taking care not to go over the outlines. Once dry (this should only take around ten minutes) dust the area with talcum powder to set the design. The henna outline will last for 2-3 weeks, but the gold will wash off easily.

Floral Midriff

For a striking midriff, try this simple floral design to frame a decorative bindi in your tummy button, It is easy to do and you can use, natural or coloured henna – for a longer lasting effect – or body paints if you only want the design for one night.

Use colours which complement the bindi you intend to use.

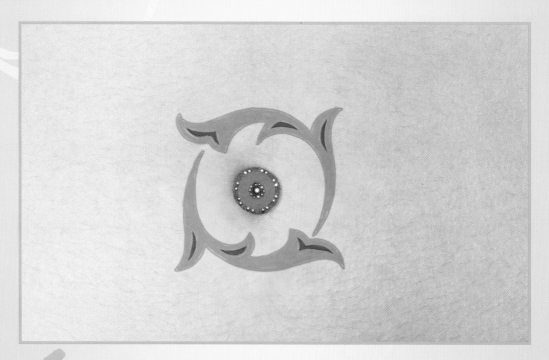

1 Wash and dry the area to be painted – do not moisturise as this may affect the staying power of the paint. Dab a light film of talcum powder over the area to be painted.

2 Trace the design onto the skin using an eyeliner – make sure that the lines are very faint.

3 Using a fine brush, draw the outline in paint. You may need to experiment with colours to find a colour that really stands out on the skin.

4 Once the outline is dry, carefully fill it in.

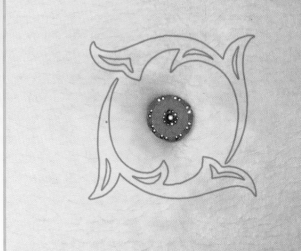

5 Set the whole design with some more talcum powder. Water based paints are temporary, so they will easily wash off.

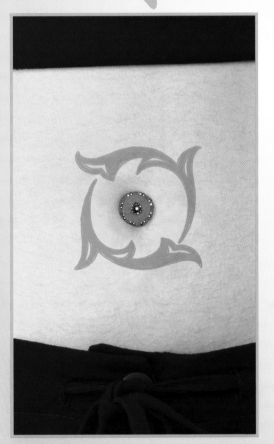

Be careful not to smudge the design when wearing it, but as long as you don't touch it, this floral design should stay in bloom all evening. For a more permanent design you can use henna and fill the colours in with alcohol based cosmetic ink.

Using Stencils with Henna

Stencils are easily available and can be used to create complex patterns anywhere on the body. Most stencils are made from soft plastic with a self-adhesive film on one side.

1 Make sure that the skin is cleansed and free of any oily residue, which may affect the adhesive quality of the the stencil.

Firmly press the stencil onto the skin, making sure that it is secure.

Spread an even layer of henna paste over the holes in the stencil – use a toothpick to push the paste into any small gaps.

Keep the henna moist with the sugar/lemon solution.

You should leave the stencil and the henna on for at least 8 hours.

When dry, peel off the stencil and wipe off the henna. Once again, use a cotton wool ball soaked in mehandi oil to remove any residue. Do not wash the area for at least 24 hours to allow the full colour to develop.

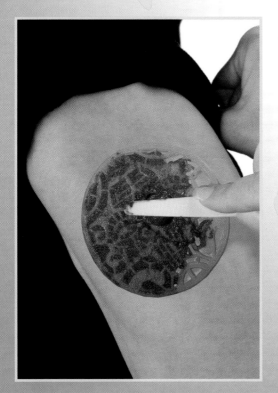

51

You can make your own stencils using waxed card or plastic and cutting out the design with a sharp craft knife. You can buy waxed card from art shops. Skin safe adhesive for the can be bought from most body art suppliers. Apply a light film of glue to the back of the stencil, press to the skin and follow the steps above.

Stencils are not recommended for use with other types of body paint, as usually the paint is very liquid and it would run underneath the stencil edges. However, you can experiment with rubber stamps.

Egyptian Symbols

Egyptian Symbols are a wonderful and rich source of possibilities for body artists. They embody a massive range of symbolic meanings and can be complex or simplistic, depending on your artistic ability and experience. For example, the symbol for a cat can be drawn as a simple outline or as a highly detailed feline form.

The colours predominantly used in Egyptian art are terracotta red, black, lapis lazuli blue and a range of pastel shades. To create these images, use henna paste, try the darker pre mixed henna paste in tubes, you can get a black that is non toxic, check with the supplier first. Red henna is also good, add beetroot juice to the henna mix to enhance the red tones.

In Egyptian times, affluent women would have lapis lazuli crystals from the Sinai Desert ground into a fine powder and then mixed with oils to produce a brilliant night sky blue colour, with flecks of gold running through it. This was used to fill in outlines and highlight detail. You can simulate this by either layering dark blue body paint with specks of metallic gold ink or you can purchase iridescent eyeshadow from theatrical suppliers.

Isis Throat Ornament

Isis was an all powerful Goddess who represented strength, mothering, fertility and wisdom in the feminine form. Associated with the moon and water, wear this symbol to enhance the regenerative powers within you. The myth of Isis centres on the resurrection and of her partner Osiris – who was cut into pieces by her jealous brother, Set. When Isis found Osiris in pieces, she was able to put him back together again and with her divine power, bring him back to life. Wear this symbol as a neck ornament to promote the powers of communication.

Use black henna or black body ink to form the outline of your design and fill in using coloured inks or body paints. Finish the effect by adding a couple of jewels glued to the design to give it extra sparkle.

We have used a design with lots of detail, but this could be simplified by cutting down on the number of feathers or the ornamental touches around the head and neck of Isis.

First make sure the area you are decorating is cleansed and prepared for your design.

Transfer your design by tracing onto a piece of tracing paper and transferring on to your skin with a brown eyeliner pencil. You could also draw the design in freehand, if you have the confidence.

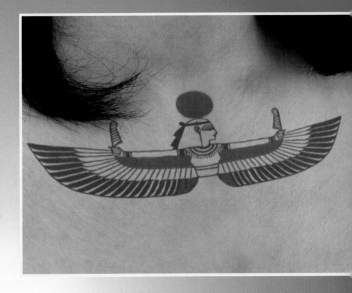

Use black henna or body ink to produce the outline – you may only need to leave the black henna on your skin for a couple of hours to get the effect needed.

Fill in the outlines with coloured inks or paints and finish the effect by highlighting details using stick on body jewels or glitter.

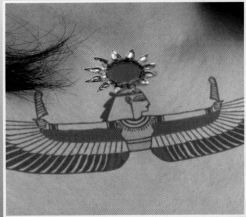

Bastet Ankle Ornament

Bastet, or Bast, is a playful cat Goddess who is either shown as a pure feline form, or as a cat headed, human female. She represents joy, pleasure, music, dancing, playfulness, agility and flirtation. Normally shown with a pierced ears or nose, the black head of Bast is a very popular and potent image. Bast worn on the ankle will lighten your step and make you want to dance!

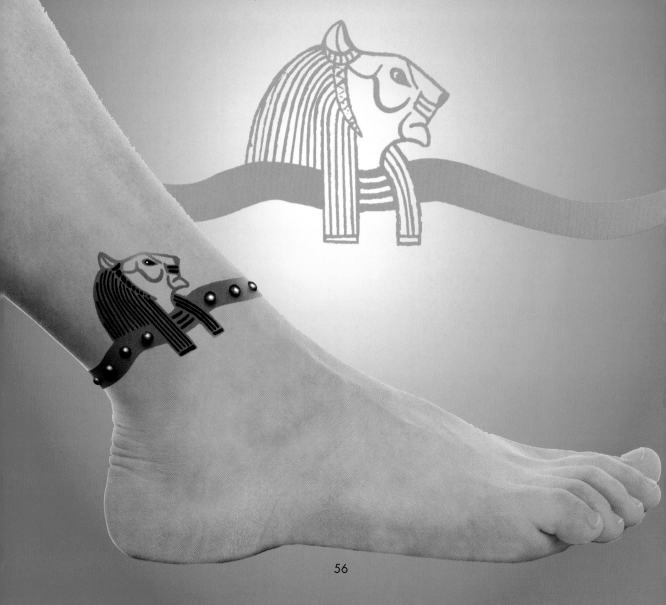

1 Begin by transferring the design onto your ankle.

2 Use natural henna applied with a thin nozzle to create the bast head and wavy anklet. Leave this on for a minimum of 8 hours so that you achieve a good dark colour.

3 Use black body paints with a fine artists brush or even a black tattoo pen to create the fine black lines, which highlight the detail on the head.

4 Allow this to thoroughly dry. Then with a clean brush put a spot of white body paint on the eye of Bast to highlight it.

5 Use stick on jewels to decorate the anklet and take these all the way around your ankle.

Make sure the jewels are glued on well with skin-safe adhesive so that they do not get dislodged while you are dancing!

57

Anubis Chest Design

Anubis was the dog or jackal headed god of the underworld. Anubis guards the soul whilst you are asleep – so that if your soul leaves your body during the night it will be able to find it's way back again. The Egyptians thought that when they died, Anubis would weigh their hearts against a feather, thus deciding their fate in the other world. This symbol should certainly be worn near the heart perhaps in conjunction with a feather, to promote balance, spiritual protection, the gift of insight and discernment.

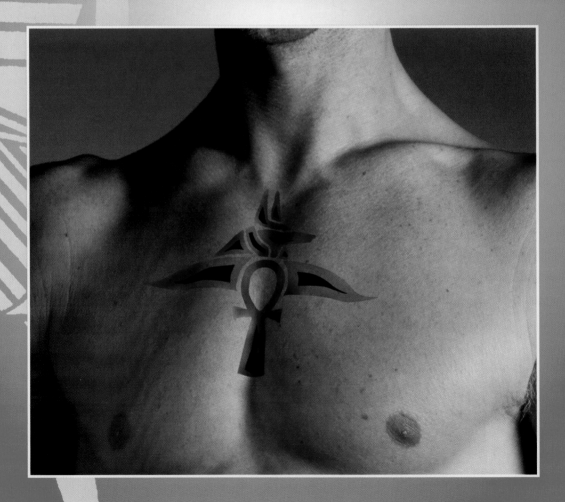

Prepare the area to be decorated in the usual way.

Use a brown eyeliner pencil to outline the design either by drawing it freehand or tracing it on to paper first.

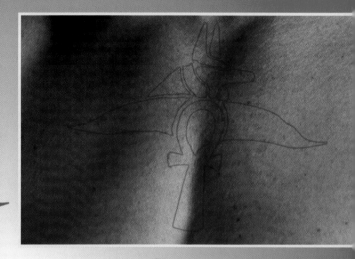

Use natural henna to outline the design first. Then, fill in the outline carefully with the henna and leave for at least 8 hours for the design to develop fully.

Remember to coat the design with the lemon juice and sugar solution to prevent it cracking.

Carefully scrape off the henna and clean with cotton wool and a little water.

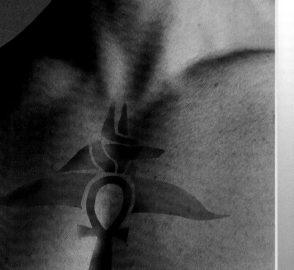

Allow it to dry thoroughly. Then, using a fine artist's brush paint in the detail with dark blue body ink or paint.

For a darker red colour to the henna you can add strong black tea to the mixture.

Scarab Hand Motif

The scarab has long been treasured as a symbol of good luck and protection. Known as 'He who came forth', wearing a scarab will promote your self confidence. Good for concentration and especially helpful if you have an examination or interview – you may have to wear this secretly, depending on your prospective employer's views on body art.

Use a dark blue henna or body dye to create the outline of the scarab motif. You can simply leave the outline or you could fill the design in using a contrasting colour.

Either trace or draw freehand the scarab outline onto the back of your hand using a dark blue tattoo pen.

Alternatively use a fine artists brush and dark blue body ink.

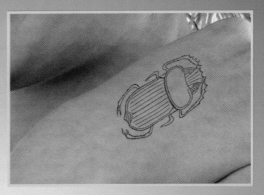

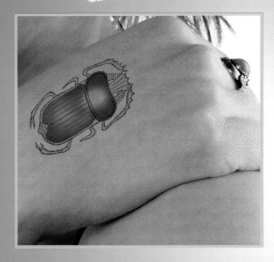

For a final touch glue a blue diamond shape jewel to the centre of the scarab and two round gold jewels – one either side of the blue one.

Do not choose jewels which stick out too far when using them in designs on your hands, as they will easily be dislodged.

Let the outline dry thoroughly. Then, carefully fill it in with blue and gold or yellow body ink.

Try to graduate the fill in colour on the body of the scarab, to give it more form.

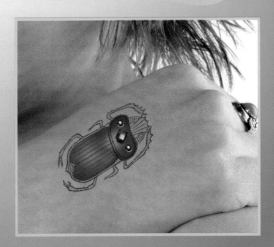

61

Art Nouveau & Organic Forms

Lovely flowing organic lines and curves. Art Nouveau lends itself beautifully to all forms of body art. You can wear these designs on almost any part of the body and, because the images are flexible, you can link several motifs together with some trailing ivy for example.

Easy to reproduce, you can paint these freehand. Try stencils or just improvise!

We suggest using body inks for these designs as the colours available are limitless. Green is used a lot, in all of it's shades, as is purple, iridescent shell colours and a hint of lavender. You can find inspiration from architectural ironwork, jewellery, ornaments and glassware from the 1920's. There are many Art Nouveau sites on the internet.

63

Floral Vine

Twist and turn the design as if it is growing up your arm. If you are confident of your ability draw it freehand for a more natural look! Worn on the upper arm or as twisting vines on the leg this design is eye-catching and dramatic, use dark red, green and gold to evoke a heady mix of decoration and decadence.

64

Flowers

Flowers are extremely feminine and powerful images. You can go for delicate daisies and forget-me-nots or more loaded symbols – such as roses or thick stemmed lilies.

A pretty pink leaf painted on the cheek bone, using body paints, is ideal for a delicate effect and stunning when highlighted with four tiny pink jewels, glued along the centre.

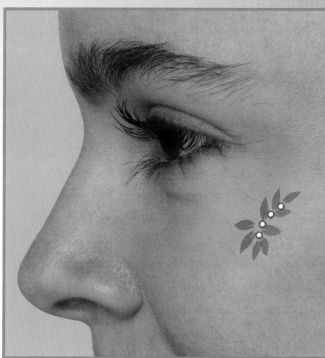

Perfect for a hot summer evening, when your shoulders are being shown off, this golden and red flower has been achieved using red body paint and gold paint over the top to outline the whole design.

65

Ivy

Ivy is a symbol of Dionysus (the Roman God of pleasure and revelry), associated with the night and powers of communication. Use green flowing lines to link other images together, or alone as a striking motif. You can use UV paint to create a glow in the dark effect under nightclub lights. This design can be worn anywhere and can be well adapted to climb and twist along your limbs – especially ankles, wrists, or as a bracelet above or below the elbow.

A band of ivy leaves just above the elbow is equally stunning for the male arm as for the female. We created this by drawing the ivy leaves freehand using green coloured henna.

Many of the coloured hennas only need to be on your skin for a couple of hours to achieve a good strong colour.

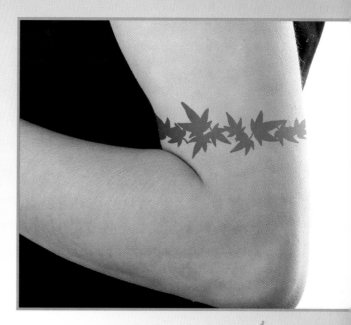

The beautiful effect below was created freehand using red body ink for the leaves. A gold body paint was used for the intertwining detail and then it was sealed with talcum powder to protect it. This design is great for an evening accessory, when you want to make the most of your midriff in the latest fashions.

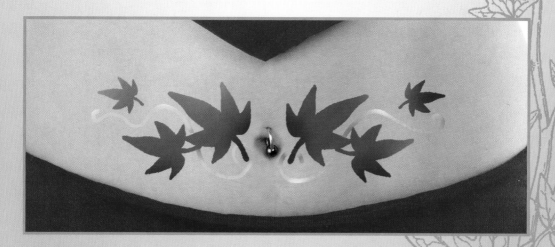

Magical Motifs

agical symbols are becoming increasingly popular. It is about reaching out beyond what you know. Magical symbols have got an immense history, which could occupy you for many lifetimes, both on the internet and on dusty library shelves. You can use all sorts of source material, from old engravings and etchings through Tarot cards right up to the Olympics and the Space program.

Here we have simply outlined 4 elements and their most popular symbols as shown in most western magic.

Chalice

The shape of a chalice, or drinking cup, is a lovely symbol for the element of water and the realm of the emotions. Use silver body paint for the cup with blue and pearlised green for the water. Apply a thin film of glitter gel to the water, and finish off the jewels on the cup with bindis and stick on gems. The chalice is a symbol of the heart, so wear this design to attract romance.

Swords

Swords have long been associated with the
element of air. The long silver blade is a
symbol of the power of mental thought. Use
silver for the blade and black for the handle.
Highlight the blade edge with white and
pale blue. Wear this design to enhance
concentration and clarity of thought.

Fire

Great for the summer, Fire is a passionate element – very energising
and positive. Use gold body paint as a base, then layer orange,
warm brown, yellow and some copper glitter over it to create a flame
that licks up your arm or down the leg, when
you want more energy and enthusiasm.

Coins

The symbol of a coin commonly represents the element of
earth. You could use a pentacle, a chinese feng shui coin or any other
coin that you like the look of. Wearing a symbol of a coin on the foot is
very grounding, and is said to attract stability and wealth. Paint the coin
shape in red first. Allow it to dry. Then, paint over it in gold.
Then, with a matchstick, gently scratch the surface of the
gold to allow a little red to show through. This should
give an authentic 'old' look to the design.

Zodiac Symbols

Twelve signs, twelve possible areas of the body, you have a ready to wear symbol that is personal to you! Try creating these with black henna outlines and then fill in with the appropriate colours as listed below.

You are not restricted as to where on the body you wear these, but here are the traditional zones associated with these signs.

Aries

Symbol: ♈

Area of body: the head

Colours: red, orange, gold

Gemini

Symbol: ♊

Area of the body: chest and throat

Colours: blue, silver, yellow

Taurus

Symbol: ♉

Area of the body: the back

Colours: brown, pink, green

Cancer

Symbol: ♋

Area of the body: breast

Colours: orange, white, green

71

Leo

Symbol: ♌

Area of body: solar plexus

Colours: yellow, gold

Libra

Symbol: ♎

Area of body: kidneys

Colours: pale green, pale blue, pale pink

Virgo

Symbol: ♍

Area of body: stomach

Colours: white, silver, denim blue

Scorpio

Symbol: ♏

Area of body: groin/sexual organs

Colours: black, red, mauve

72

Sagittarius

Symbol: ♐

Area of body: thighs and legs

Colours: red, copper, bronze

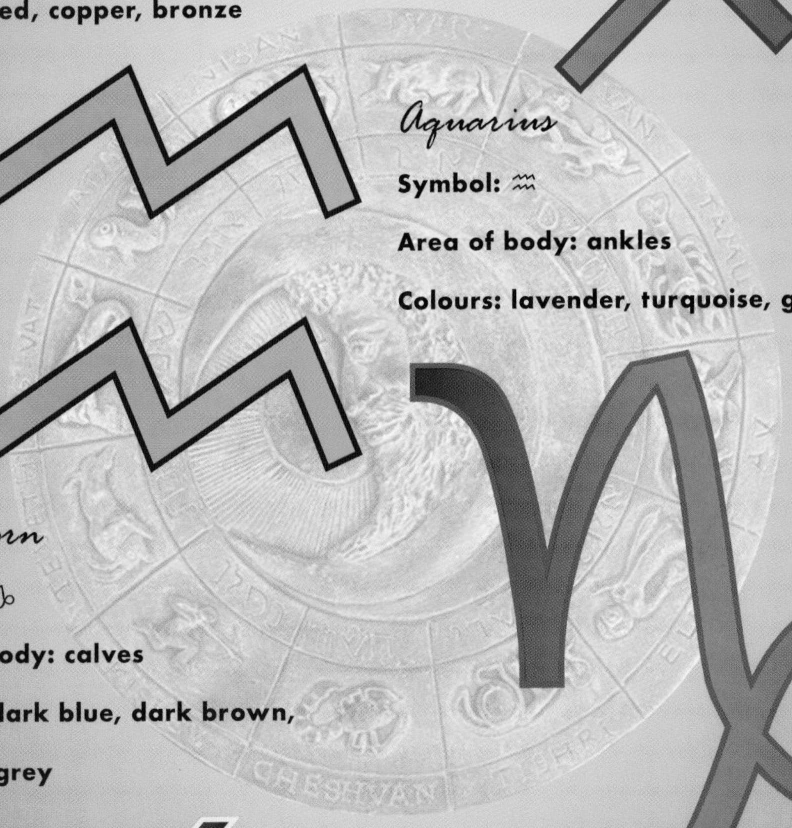

Aquarius

Symbol: ♒

Area of body: ankles

Colours: lavender, turquoise, green

Capricorn

Symbol: ♑

Area of body: calves

Colours: dark blue, dark brown, charcoal grey

Pisces

Symbol: ♓

Area of body: feet

Colours: green, silver, purple

When we think of body art we normally think of tattoos and when we think of tattoos we often conjure up stereotype images of sailors with anchors, parrots and beautiful women tattooed onto their arms. Either that or we face images of punk rockers with pierced everything and shocking motifs adorning every bare piece of flesh. These examples are extreme, but similar effects can be achieve with kinder and not so permanent consequences. With body paints and henna, the basic colours which are used in traditional tattoos can be mimicked and some great fun effects can be achieved.

The following ideas can be achieved using henna or body paint – or a mixture of the two. The main thing to remember is that they all have thick black outlines to give them the heavy traditional look.

Add bright green and yellow for more sophisticated versions. Many pop stars wear traditional old style tattoos, deliberately bright and gaudy for a kitsch effect!

Examples:

Swallows on the shoulder blade.

Heart on the bosom or upper arm.

Mermaid on the upper arm.

Anchor lower inner arm.

Rose on the bosom or upper arm.

Classic Symbols

*T*he range of symbols is vast, but, remember, each symbol has it's own meaning and it's own unique energy. Choose positive symbols to promote wellbeing and individuality. Symbols are very powerful, so have fun researching the images that represent what you wish to attract in your life!

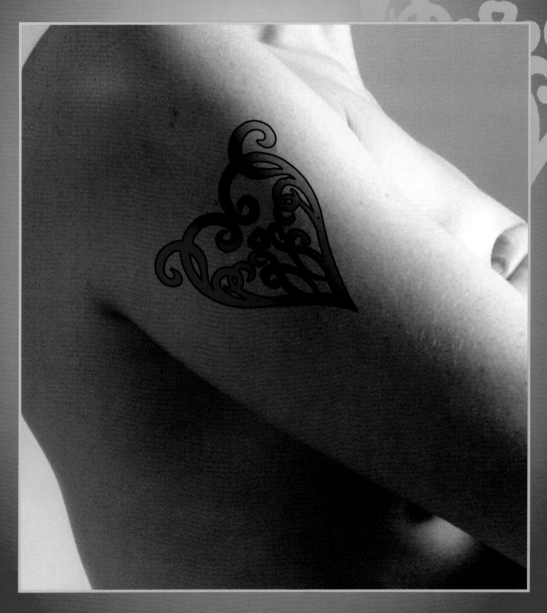

There are many books on symbolism available. Also look at coats of arms, company logos and most importantly, your dreams! There are always particular images that you are drawn to, so why not paint them on your body. Experiment with various mediums to create the effect that you want.

Crowns, thorns, barbed wire, feathers, keys, dragons, birds, butterflies, etc – all make excellent subjects.

Writing & Calligraphy

*T*he notion of writing on the body has been made popular in recent years through films like Peter Greenaway's 'The Pillow Book'. Why not try painting calligraphy on your own body, or that of a friend.

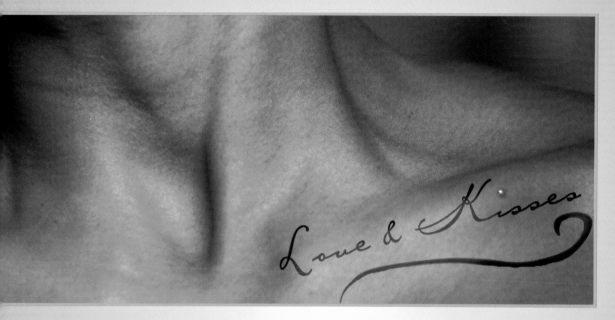

You can experiment with different types of brushes and simply paint body ink on, with loose, improvised strokes, or more controlled calligraphic skill. Take inspiration from poetry and song lyrics. Also check out the multiple forms of calligraphy as they have been used over the ages. Many cultures have developed very sophisticated forms of lettering, so it is well worth doing some research.

Try Chinese, Runic, Hindu, Arabic bands.
These bands are simply made up of
random letters from exotic alphabets, or if
you prefer, use translations of energising
words like JOY, POWER, LOVE,
BEAUTIFUL, STRONG. Simply paint the
letters on in freehand, either using henna
or inks, in circles around ankles, wrists,
arms, legs, neck and even the waist!

79

Sun & Moon

The Sun and Moon have always been associated with masculine and feminine energies respectively. The Moon is said to reflect the Sun's brightness, at the same time as having it's own particular power – which is that of the subconscious and intuitive feelings.

The Sun is a bright, energising and life giving star, that brings clarity, optimism and warmth. Although they are very popular and well used, these two magical symbols are both natural, primal and essentially the most powerful images of all. You can choose whether to go for impact or subtlety. A little

Moon on your ear lobe or a huge Sun on your back, it's up to you. Use warm shades like yellow, gold, orange, red and metallic gold, bronze and copper, for the Sun. Pale blue, dark blue, purple, glittery silvers and iridescent powders, for the Moon.

Egyptian Hand Motif
Eye of Horus and the Eye of Re.

In very early times, Egyptians regarded the Sun and the Moon to be the eyes of the great falcon headed god Horus. The left eye was called the 'Eye of Horus' and was a symbol of the Moon. The right eye was known as the 'Eye of Re', and was a symbol of the Sun.

You can wear one on each wrist, thus balancing the male and female energies. Keep the outlines strong and fill in with rich glittery blues and gold.

Traditional Sun and Moon

The smiling face of the sun and the sleeping moon have been used for centuries on old maps and in illustrations. They are particularly nice when reproduced one on each shoulder blade or on the upper arm.

They can be worn as a pair or on their own.

They are often seen in a sepia colour, so they would look good when simply done with natural henna.

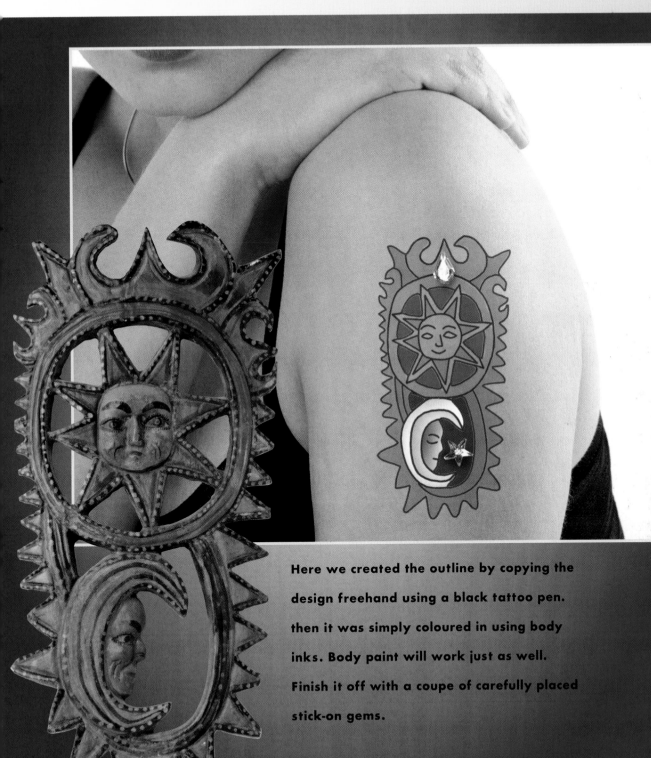

Here we created the outline by copying the design freehand using a black tattoo pen. then it was simply coloured in using body inks. Body paint will work just as well. Finish it off with a coupe of carefully placed stick-on gems.

83

Fruit

What do we think of when we think of fruit? Well, it is natural, colourful, nutritious, healthy and energising. Fruit is symbolic of life and life force. From the apple to the pomegranate, from advertising to the Garden of Eden, fruit is literally full of intrigue. A cherry on the forearm for example, symbolises "my cherry!" as in my love, my darling, my sweet. A hot red Mexican chilli on the back of the calf symbolises "I'm hot stuff!" as in wild, daring and fun. Whereas, the simple apple, seems to embody both "apple pie" as in homely, devoted and wholesome emotions as well as the more potent story of Eve in the Garden of Eden.

Look through magazines and old Victorian illustrations for inspiration.

Examples:

A pair of cherries on the outer fore arm.

A red chilli pepper on the back of the calf.

An apple on the sole of the feet.

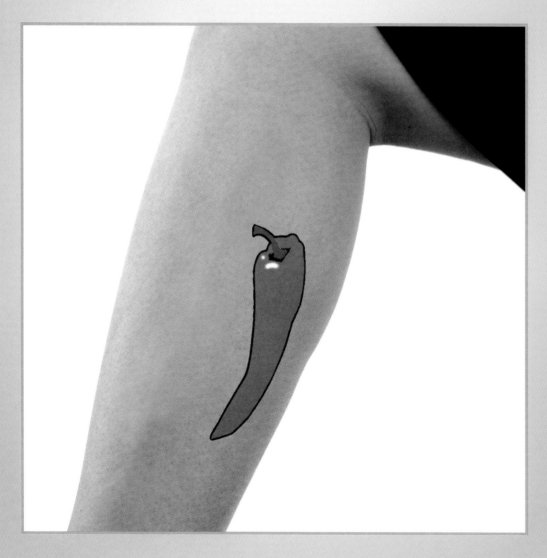

Goddesses & Gods

Male and Female energy forms, that are interchangeable and all powerful, are represented by Gods and Goddesses. Each God or Goddess carries with them a range of attributes unique to them, whether it be healing, life giving or inspiring – the range of possibilities is awesome. Look at different religions and explore the vast amount of information available, both on the internet and in mythology.

Finding the right image can be very satisfying and every God or Goddess has their own story, which you can relate to your friends when you display your body art.

Goddesses

A Sphinx on the shoulder blade would give you a mysterious air, add a shimmer of gold powder over the design to add extra depth.

If you are expecting a child or would like to conceive, a Fertility goddess gently drawn on the tummy is a loving expression of feminine energy. Use soft orange, browns and pearlised white.

A Celtic battle Goddess on the arm gives you confidence and strength. This is a particularly good motif to wear if you are going through a difficult time. Use blue, silver and black.

Gods

Thor's lightning bolt on your chest or arm will give you

courage and confidence. Use silver and blue.

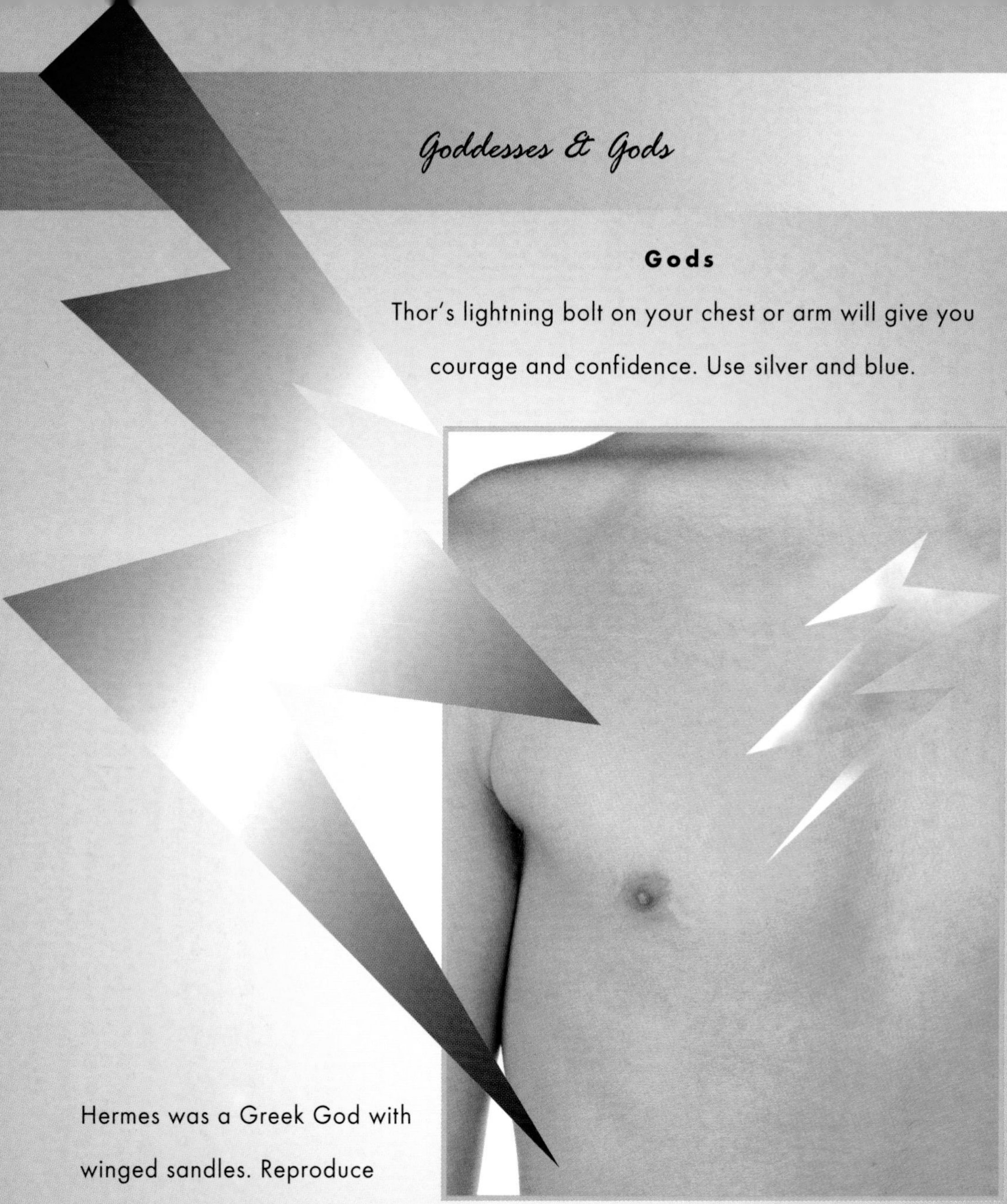

Hermes was a Greek God with

winged sandles. Reproduce

one of these on your own ankle to promote

communication skills and give your social life a

boost!

Apollo, the Sun God, worn on the chest acts as a protective shield, as well as instilling

confidence and creativity. Use gold and orange.

Science fiction films, heavily influence both clubbers and catwalks. Films like 'Star Wars', 'Star Trek' and 'Blade Runner' use stunning visual effects to make people seem alien or unusual. Look through comics, watch films, check out adverts to find interesting futuristic looks. Don't be afraid to experiment with the unconventional – you will have a lot of fun along the way.

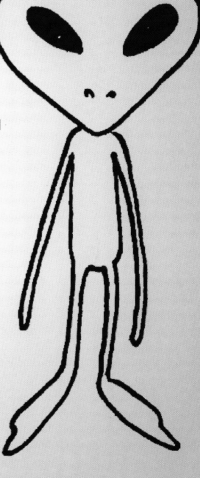

The internet has many sites devoted to the alien species in Science Fiction films – most of which simply use strange markings to differentiate them from other species. Take a look at Judzia Dax from 'Star Trek', she has small leopard skin spots running down her face and neck. Queen Amidala from Star Wars Episode 1 wears specific regal makeup to increase her status and power. Mystique from the 'X Men' film has blue body paint all over her and the look is completed with coloured contact lenses. Be as daring as you want to be – you will definitely get noticed!

Useful Information

Body Art Supply

16016 SE Division

Ste. 149, Portland,

Oregon 97236

U.S.A.

www.bodyartsupply.com

Supplier of extensive range of henna and other body art products including natural and coloured henna pastes and powders, temporary transfer tattoos, plastic and multi tat stencils and accessories to enhance your designs – take a look at their website it contains an online catalogue with their full range of products.

Mehndi Body Art/the Bomb Factory

2501 E. 28th Street

Suite 118

Signal Hill

California

www.mehndibodyart.com

Supplier of henna and other temporary body art products. Also has an internet body art gallery

Mehndi Madness

2211 NW Market Street

Seattle

WA 206 782 7314

Established henna and Mehndi stockist. Internet web page includes gallery, designs and kits as well as interactive classes.

Marsh Morgan

Ash Hill Court

Ash Hill Road

Torquay

Devon

TQ1 3JD

www.webtribe.net

Innovative body artist with internet body art gallery page. Also a supplier of body art materials

Halawa henna

ESS House

94-6 Chapel Street

Leigh

Lancashire

www.halawahenna.demon.co.uk

Supplier of henna body art products. Also has gallery page on Internet with more traditional bias.

Many high street store supply body art products so check out your local stores for easy access.

Remember to always read the packaging and instructions that come with the products. Check the ingredients listing on the products – if it doesn't have one don't buy it! Always patch test products on your skin before going ahead with a design and if you have any allergic reaction at all don't use it.

Index